MOSES KORIR

MOSES
AND THE
IMPOSSIBLE
PIANO

Archway Publishing books may be ordered through booksellers or by contacting:

Archway Publishing
1663 Liberty Drive
Bloomington, IN 47403
www.archwaypublishing.com
844-669-3957

ISBN: 978-1-6657-5203-9 (sc)
ISBN: 978-1-6657-5204-6 (e)

Library of Congress Control Number: 2023920281

Print information available on the last page.

Archway Publishing rev. date: 11/14/2023

I was born under the shadow of Mount Elgon, a great extinct volcano in northwestern Kenya.

I am a Kalenjin, of the Nilotic people, or people of the Nile River, the longest river in all of Africa.

When I was a boy, my days were made up of going to school, tending the cattle, and working in the garden alongside my 7 brothers and sisters.

But once my chores were done, my friends and I would roam, and run, and wrestle until our legs gave out and our eyes began to droop. And then we would fall in a heap on the floor wherever we were; a great mountain of happy, sleeping children.

Life in my village was very good, but nothing could have prepared me for the excitement of attending my first Pathfinder campout with children from my village. We crowded into a Matatu and headed out on our adventure.

We saw monkeys climbing in the trees and deer grazing in the grasslands.

As the Matatu sped down the road my friend shouted, "Look! The trees are running away!". We all laughed at the image in our heads.

Our camp was in a big open field and would be attended by more than 3000 children.

We found our campsite and helped our teachers set up the tents.

The air was full of the Laughter and shouting of so many children enjoying the many camp activities. There was sack racing, and swimming, and hide and seek, and drills, and marching, and singing, and gymnastics, and going on forest adventures. We were eager to finish our task so that we could add our voices to the noise.

While preparing our campsite I heard the most wonderful sound that I had ever heard before.

"What is that?" I asked my teacher.

"It is music played on a piano" she responded.

"What is a piano?" I asked.

"Something with black and white keys" she answered.

I did not know what these keys were but the sound they made wrapped around me like a big hug; I knew I had to find the source.

Under the spell of the musical notes, I left my group and followed the sound. Maybe I would find a great big radio, or maybe these keys would open a door. Or maybe a zebra; zebras were black and white!

I ran all the way to the arena and maneuvered my way through the many children to the stage at the very center. And there it was, the thing with the black and white keys, a piano!

"No kids are allowed around this place!", the man warned, and he shoo'd the children away. I sadly moved back to watch and listen from afar.

Suddenly my teacher appeared in front of me. "Moses!", she exclaimed. "Why did you run away? We still have work to do on our campsite". I was so sad to leave but also so happy to have seen a piano for the first time.

The next morning, I woke up early. I showered and ate my breakfast quickly so that I could be the first one at the arena for the best view of the podium.

I was greeted by the same man from the day before. "Kids are not allowed around the podium; go away!", he warned again. But I still stood as close as I could to the piano.

The next morning and all the mornings for the whole week I would do the same thing; quickly shower, quickly eat, run to the front of the arena, be told to "Go away!" by the man at the piano, but inch as close as I could to it.

As we packed and got ready to go home, I knew my life had changed forever; Our drive home seemed more beautiful, the trees seemed to run faster, there were more deer and monkeys, and I was now a pianist; there was only one thing missing…

"Mummy, mummy! I must have a piano!", I yelled as I ran through the front door of our muddy hut.

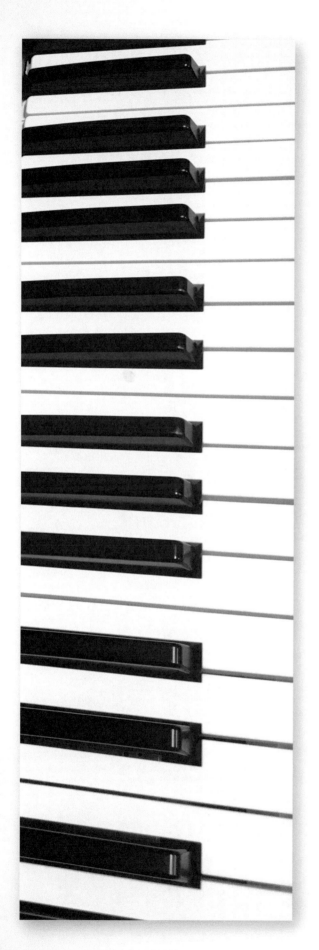

"What is a piano?" my mother asked.

"It is something with black and white keys", I answered.

"Something with black and white keys?", she puzzled out loud.

The next day at school I asked each of my friends if they knew of a piano. "It is something with black and white keys", I told them.

Everyone laughed and looked at me like I was a silly monkey and said, "we have never heard of that before".

Then one day, after a long asking and searching for a piano, one of my friends came to me at school and said, "Moses, my father has just returned from Sudan and has brought with him something with black and white stripes, and it might be what you have been looking for".

I couldn't believe my ears. Could this be a piano? I took a deep breath to calm my excited, racing heart and waited impatiently for school to end.

Word of this new discovery quickly spread among my friends, and as soon as school was over, we ran as a group to see this thing with black and white stripes!

It was a piano! And in my very own village. And the man let me take it home.

We stopped at the closest shop to buy batteries, and then rushed to my house to try the new piano.

"Can you play it, Moses? Can you play a song?", they asked anxiously.

And without hesitation I responded, "Yes! I am a pianist!". Everyone cheered as I played my first song.

That was a long time ago. Now I am a father with two pianists of my own, a teacher of many children, and the owner of two pianos. The lesson that I have learned is when something seems impossible, maybe it is possible. You'll never know… unless you try.

Printed in the United States
by Baker & Taylor Publisher Services